DK

Discover more at
www.dk.com

Illustrations by
Jonathan Heale

This American edition, 2006
06 07 10 9 8 7 6 5 4 3 2 1

Published in the United States by
Dorling Kindersley Pub lishing Inc., 375 Hudson Street
New York, New York 10014

Photography (Title page penguins; page 10
orangutan; page 12 jaguar; page 15 toucan, camel;
page 19 tiger cub; page 20 jaguar; Jacket tiger cub)
copyright © 1991 Philip Dowell
Photography (Imprint page butterfly; page 7 cockatoo, wolf;
page 9 duck; page 10 butterfly; page 12 ladybugs; page 13 fish;
page 14 rhinoceros, fox, crocodile; page 16 ladybug)
copyright © 1991 Jerry Young
Photography (page 8 polar bear) copyright © 1992 Jerry Young
Photography (Title page rabbit kittens; page 11 rabbit;
page 18 rabbit; page 19 rabbit kittens; page 20 duck)
copyright © 1991 Barrie Watts

ISBN: 0756621801

CIP data for this title
is available.

Color reproduction
by Colourscan
Printed inChina by
Leo Paper Products

my first book of
animals

Roger Priddy

What do I say?

kitten

Meow

donkey

Ee-aW
Ee-aW

Ooo
Ooo
Ooo

chimpanzee

calves

Moooo
Moooo

cockatoo

Howwlll

wolf

Squark Squark

pig

hen
and
chicks

Oink oink

Cluck
Cluck

Cheep-cheep-cheep-cheep-cheep-cheep

What we say

dog

Woof Woof

Grrowll

Baaa Baaa sheep

Squeak-squeak-squeak-squeak

mouse

polar bear

QuackQuack

duck

WhOo WhOOoo

owls

Neighhh

horse

Rrroarrr

lion

9

Animal colors

blue
butterfly

red
parrot

orange orangutan

black panther

brown bear

white rabbit

green lizard

yellow
ducklings

Spotted animals

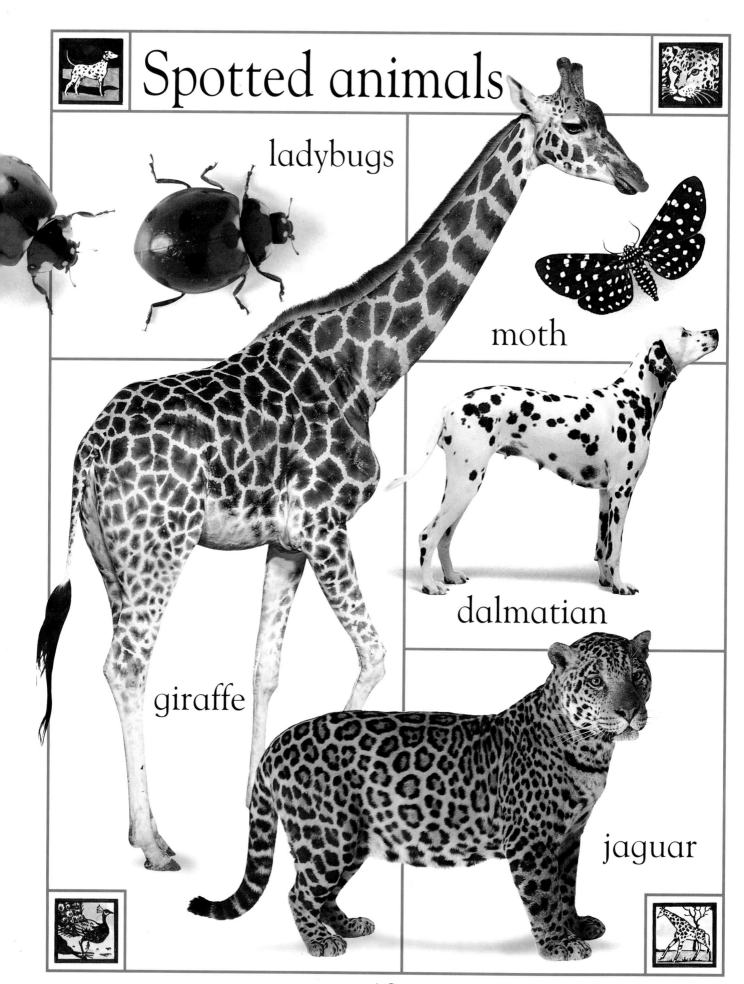

ladybugs

moth

dalmatian

giraffe

jaguar

Striped animals

tigers

chipmunk

zebra

fish

Animal features

A flamingo has a long neck and long legs.

This rhinoceros has horns on its nose.

A porcupine is very prickly.

This fox has very big ears.

A crocodile has lots of sharp teeth.

14

A toucan has a big beak.

An elephant has a long trunk.

This camel has a hump.

A kangaroo has a long tail and very big back feet.

Creepy crawlies

wasp

butterfly

moth

bee

ladybug

damselfly

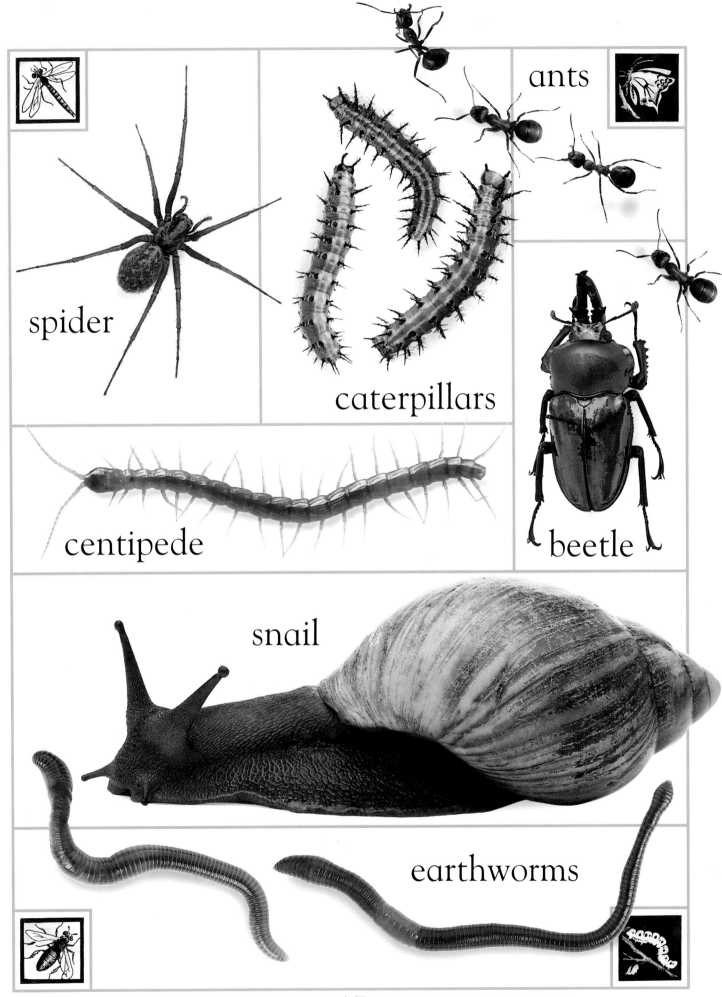

ants

spider

caterpillars

beetle

centipede

snail

earthworms

Find my baby

tiger

sheep

dog

giraffe

hen

rabbit

puppies

lamb

rabbit kittens

chicks

giraffe calf

tiger cub

19

Find more babies

leopard

cow

pig

zebra

cat

duck

kittens

piglet

duckling

leopard
cub

calf

zebra
foal

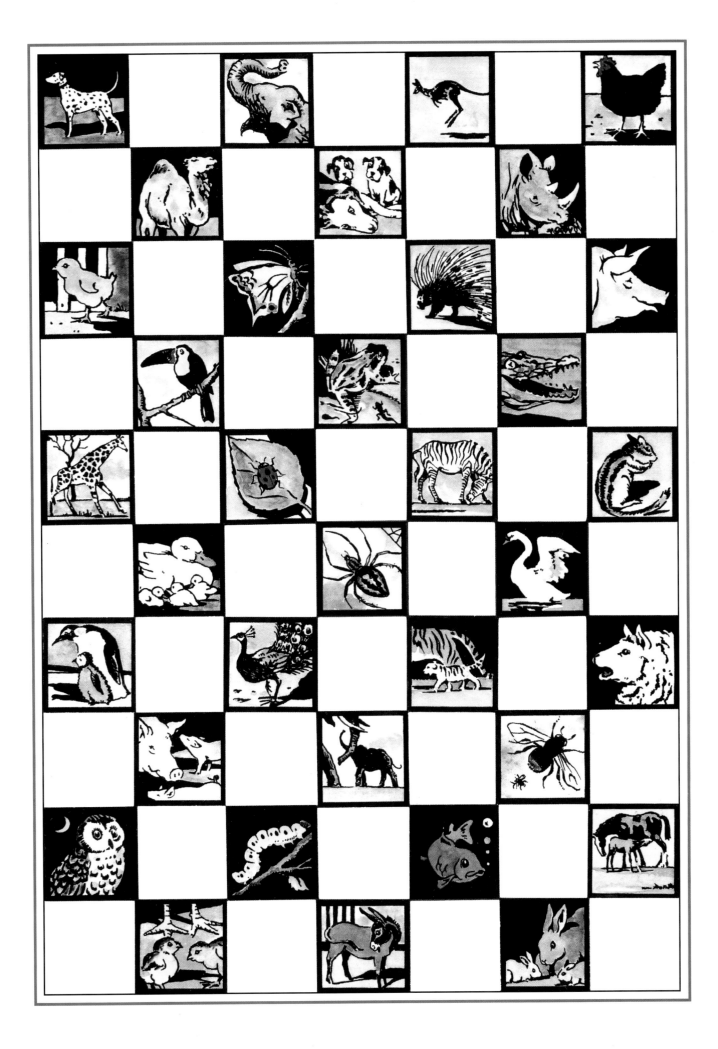